To my best friend, Aaron. You
light up my world. Thank you for
always encouraging, supporting,
challenging and lifting me up.
And thank you for the laughter.
Life is so fun - with you in it.

© 2020 Louie's Little Lessons and Elizabeth A. Fletcher
www.louieslittlelessons.com

All rights reserved. No part of this publication may be reproduced, distributed, or transmitted in any form or by any means, including photocopying, recording, or other electronic or mechanical methods, without the prior written permission of the publisher, except in the case of brief quotations embodied in critical reviews and certain other noncommercial uses permitted by copyright law.

Books may be purchased in quantity and/or special sales by contacting the publisher, Louie's Little Lessons, at hello@louieslittlelessons.com.

Published in San Diego, California by Louie's Little Lessons. Louie's Little Lessons is a registered trademark.

Illustrations by: Greg Bishop
Interior Design by: Ron Eddy
Cover Design by: Greg Bishop and Ron Eddy
Editing by: Julie Breihan

Printed in China

ISBN: 978-0-9981936-6-3

Louie's Little Lessons

THERE'S A BABY IN THE HOUSE

written by **Liz Fletcher**   illustrated by **Greg Bishop**

Louie is an elephant hero,
Saving the world by night and day.

He's brave, courageous, and kind
And he also loves to play.

Building blocks are his favorite.
Arts and crafts are great too!
He's super-fast on his scooter.
What do you like to do?

Louie loves being a hero.
It takes a lot of bravery, you know.
But lately he's been lonely
and feeling a little low.

Louie wishes he had a friend,
Cause you can't play catch with just one.

And there's no teeter without a totter.
He needs another superhero to have fun.

Daddy says a new baby is coming.
Louie doesn't know what to do.

Is their house big enough for all of them?
Can't the baby just live at the zoo?

Louie has so many questions.
He's not sure where to start.
Will baby get all the attention?
Can Mommy share her heart?

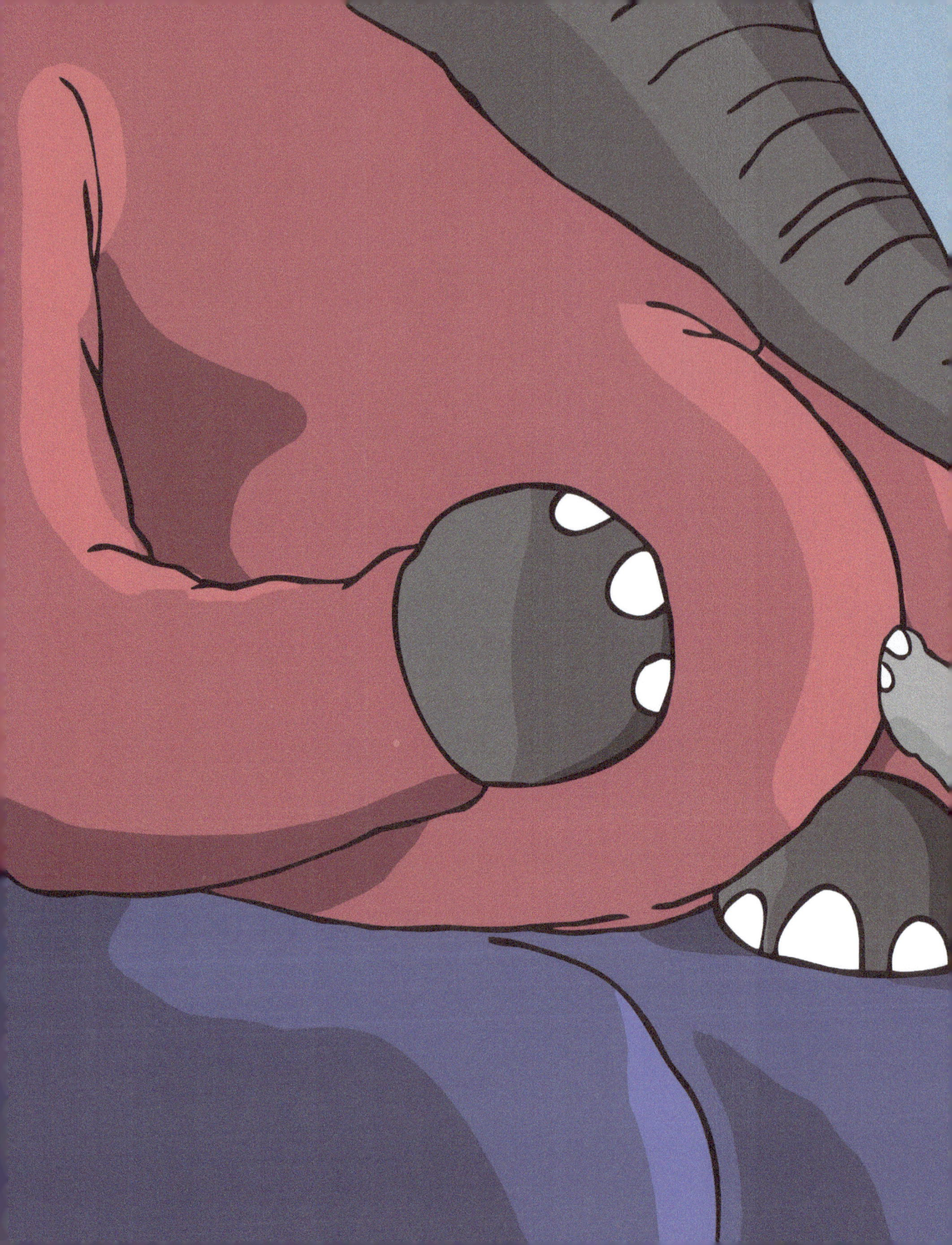

Hmm, Louie thinks.
He's unsure of this big change.
*I'm only used to what I know
So this feels kinda strange.*

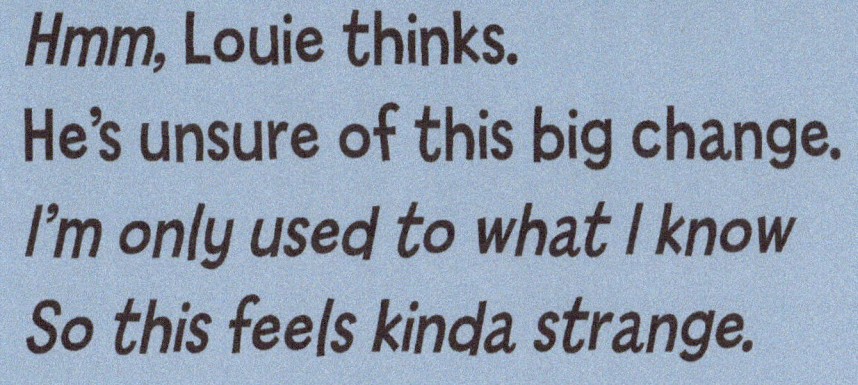

Louie grabs his cape tightly.
He can feel his confidence grow.

What am I so afraid of?
he thinks.

New adventures await,
let's go!

"We're aliens from a faraway planet,
Discovering new lands and places.
We like Earth the best, I think.
Look! So many welcoming faces!"

"The kitchen is our playground,
My sous chef and I.

Voilà! Look at our masterpiece!
It's a chocolatey chocolate mousse pie!"

Because the only thing more powerful than one superhero is two!

"Having a new baby is great!
I'm the older sibling, you see.
My job is very important,
And no one can do it but me."

Louie helps with nap time and diapers
and gives lots of kisses and cuddles.
Baby needs time to grow and get big
So one day they can jump in rain puddles!

The love in Louie's heart is bigger,
And there's enough for everyone.

"I have a best friend to play with,
 And the days are packed full of fun!"

Change can be exciting.
Louie's glad he loves someone new.
He adores his growing family,
And you know what? You will too!

www.ingramcontent.com/pod-product-compliance
Lightning Source LLC
Chambersburg PA
CBHW040752020526
44118CB00042B/2927